FIRE HR NOW!

Working with HR
to shape up **or** ship out

Lori Kleiman, SPHR

ISBN: 149283257X
ISBN 13: 9781492832577
Library of Congress Control Number: 2013920156
CreateSpace Independent Publishing Platform, North Charleston, SC

ACKNOWLEDGEMENTS

This book is a culmination of my consulting career, from the view of an HR administrator, business owner and consultant. A career in human resources is born from years of education, experiences, patience, exasperation, ambition and study of the human spirit. I could not have undertaken such a journey over the past 25 years without the support of family and friends that believed in the goals that I set, even if they seemed risky, when far simpler paths were available.

My clients over the last 20 years have graciously allowed me into their inner circle. For many, our relationship went past that of vendor, and we created a collaborative friendship to move all our businesses forward. Their stories are shared with confidence, but as you recognize your story, know it is included with the utmost respect that I have for your business and our years working together. I thank you for your relationship through the years.

The path that lead to this book would not have been possible if not for the unconditional support from my husband Andy Korn, and our three amazing children. My parents and sister were with me full speed ahead as I made life changing moves that gathered the stories and expertise you read in this book.

Libby Snow participated with her graduate school expertise, analysis of the quotes for each chapter and helping select the final artwork and layout. She is a sounding board that I always rely on for a critical perspective.

The initial impetus and encouragement to craft the book came from my dear friend and colleague Joe Wert. Only with his quick feedback and ongoing gut check did I take the risk to move forward. And for the courage to retain such a provocative title, I thank Clay Garner, once my Vistage chair, always my friend and mentor.

Friends play a critical part in every move we make, and without the encouragement of Susan Spritz Myers and Annie and Ross Rutherford, I may never have had the courage that it took to take the plunge allowing me the

ACKNOWLEDGEMENTS

time and freedom to write. Thanks to all three of you for being there when I needed it most.

Last and most importantly, my editor, Marjorie Korn. This book allowed me to see Marjorie at work first hand. Her ability to provide constructive feedback and enhance the syntax elevated this book to a very special place. She was able to attain a balance between my conversational writing style and her background as a journalist and editor that you see here. Working with Marjorie has been my greatest pleasure, and one I will never forget.

TABLE OF CONTENTS

CHAPTER 1

WHERE ARE WE TODAY?

"HR is the corporate function with the greatest potential — the key driver, in theory, of business performance — and also the one that most consistently under delivers."

Keith Hammond's article, Why We Hate HR.
Fast Company, 2005

Chief executive officers seem content to have a human resources function that is underperforming and draining resources rather than adding to the bottom line. Why is it tolerated? You have every right to expect your HR executive to be decisive, innovative and responsive. The HR team must have a firm grip on your business based on a foundation of human resources. While the passion for HR may be its base, the HR business partner for your management team must be an executive first and HR professional second. In this role, the expectation is one of presenting solutions for business issues with facts and data that will support organizational buy-in, growth and success.

This book is for CEOs who are frustrated with the administrative and bureaucratic actions of their human resources department. At the same time, we want to provide the HR executive insight into the issues CEOs are considering around the HR function. Most organizations feel they must have HR but can't see any value they add to the bottom line. We aim to show the CEO what HR can provide, and help the CEO decide whether your HR executive can take you where you need to go. With a dual purpose, this book has a secondary goal of sending a constructive message to HR executives to shape up or ship out. In an effort to get HR on the same page, we include a memo at the end of each chapter for HR executives who want to meet the expectations of their CEO and make a meaningful impact within their organization.

Human resources will generally take on responsibility for the full cycle of employment: from initial contact with candidates, to the separation from the organization, including ongoing communication with employees that are no longer formally affiliated with the organization. The size of the organization changes the dynamics of the HR function. In a very small organization, the position may be the responsibility of an office manager, chief financial officer, or other administrative team member. In larger organizations there will be a team of human resource professionals ranging from administrative or clerical personnel to the senior vice president level. If the title of the book was interesting to the CEO, then the current HR executive needs to take notice regardless of the size of the organization. In a small organization, the HR executive will be looking to understand what they need to do to take HR to the next level, while in larger organizations the leader of the HR function will use the content to evaluate their department as well as consider if their professional goals are aligned with the goals of the CEO. For the purposes of this book, we will refer to the most senior person responsible for the HR function as the HR executive, understanding this person may have a different title in your organization.

HR, as we know it today, is the grandchild of the human relations movement, which began in the early 20th century with pioneering work by Frederick Taylor in lean manufacturing. Taylor explored what he termed "scientific management," striving to improve economic efficiency in manufacturing jobs. He eventually identified one of the principal inputs into the manufacturing process — labor — which sparked others to look more closely at workforce productivity.

A well-known pioneer in the study of labor in the workplace was Elton Mayo, whose Hawthorne studies documented how employees reacted when they were provided various stimuli. The work of the Hawthorne Studies found that when employees were the focus of attention, suddenly productivity increased. Unrelated to financial compensation and working conditions, the experiment concluded that attention and engagement were the factors that yield more productive workers.

From the Hawthorne studies, business owners concluded if they had systems in place that provided an emphasis on employees, the positive relationship created would yield higher productivity and quality. This highlighted management's need for a position that would focus on workers. In the mid-twentieth century, the position of personnel administrator was created in many manufacturing operations. This was the foundation upon which human resources departments of the latter part of the 20th century were created.

The early personnel departments were very tactical in nature. Their primary focus was to meet the needs of the employees and provide administrative services for the organization. In general, the personnel department was seen as an administrative function requiring clerical and customer service skills. HR departments have evolved to be the shepherd of the culture of their organizations. Today, executives in high performing organizations rely on HR to drive business initiatives and ensure corporate programs are sustainable throughout the organization.

We see HR departments that run the gamut from purely administrative groups to fully engaged business professionals that move the mission of the enterprise forward. What is best for your organization is based on the culture you desire, the needs of the management team, and the ability to engage and retain a workforce that meets your mission.

The competitive advantage of business is often aligned with the initiatives seen in popular culture. Throughout the past fifty years, we have seen changes in cultural priorities, and the way businesses go to market has changed as well. The chart below reflects changes in cultural and business focus since the 1960s. Can you see a similar evolution in your organizational movement from then until now?

Today's business world must embrace human capital for all the value it brings and use advances in processes and technology as the building blocks upon which our employees can embrace organizational goals and move forward. Your top HR executive must understand this evolution to be a driving force in your business. We will explore why you need an engaged HR executive and how the right team under that person can be a critical and vibrant component of your enterprise. There is no "right way" to embrace HR; it must fit with the other departments in your organization. At the same time, you as the CEO must understand the value HR can bring and make decisions about the purpose of

HR that is right for your team. Through the evaluation and reflection provided in this book, you will ensure that you have an HR function that is supportive of your organizational culture and goals.

CEOs have to run their business, and have often viewed HR as an administrative function that they needed, a place for employees to go so managers can manage. When speaking with CEOs, we often hear comments regarding HR that sound like:

- HR departments cost money and they spend the day telling managers what they can't do.
- HR is responsible for the necessary evils of business.
- We'd all be happy if HR just stayed in their office and kept employees from complaining all day.
- What is this nonsense about wanting a seat at the table? There is no table: the management team directs, accounting pays bills, operations produces products, and marketing sells them.

If this is how you feel, you're not alone. The goal of this book is to highlight the value HR can bring to your organization, and help you evaluate whether its inclusion in management is right for you. For some businesses, HR should have only a limited, administrative function. If that's the case, we will explore options that help you move HR to an outsourced relationship, so you can ultimately *FIRE HR NOW!* But for many, the right HR team can be transformative, adding value to the top and bottom line of your operation on a daily basis.

HOW BIG IS BIG ENOUGH?

A senior living community with 600 employees has all HR tasks handled by the accounting function. There are three HR administrators that report directly to the CFO. All have been with the organization over twenty years, and work in a part time or shared capacity. In an initial conversation with the CFO, he stated, "we aren't really big enough to have a dedicated HR manager." When the consultant clarified the size of the organization, the CFO was shocked to know that most organizations their size do in fact have dedicated HR. The clerical piece of the HR puzzle was being completed, but there was no strategic alignment around talent, and the compliance piece was left for each department to handle on their own. This is a case where we would recommend you FIRE HR NOW! and rebuild the function with talent that can help move the organization forward.

How you will incorporate HR into your organization will be a strategic decision. To make the best decision, you must understand the various components that account for the HR function we will be addressing in the text. Specifically, how can you utilize HR to drive your mission forward and ensure you have the talent and bench strength to meet the future goals of your organization?

Essentially, HR is responsible for the life cycle of the employee. In most organizations, this starts with a potential candidate and ends with separation. The chart below provides a baseline for the HR department in most organizations to ensure a common understanding of its responsibilities. This is where our reflection begins.

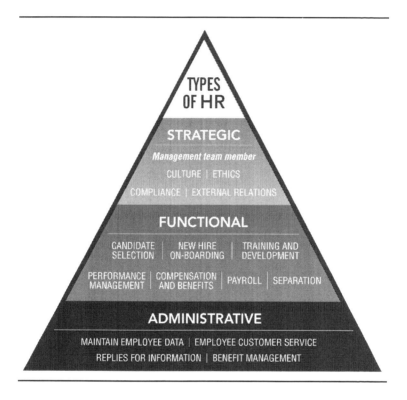

The goal of HR isn't simply getting people in seats and administering payroll and benefits. If that is the case in your organization, you're missing the real value of an HR department. Sure, your HR department can be strictly administrative, but we will argue that the risk of that is great, and the rewards you forego are plentiful. Instead, demand the same business-minded excellence you require from your other strategic functions and use human resources as your competitive advantage.

There is also increasing diversity in the way work is accomplished. Contractors, part-time workers, and tele-commuters are all viable options available in the workforce. According to a Deloitte study entitled "Human Capital Trends 2013," we are in an "open talent economy – a collaborative, transparent, technology-driven, rapid-cycle way of doing business." There are solid business reasons to embrace these new workplace trends. The study goes on to acknowledge the workload of the CEO is, and encourage the HR executive to take the reins on bringing these work arrangements into the organization. The concepts need to be evaluated against the goals of the organization where they make sense. The HR executive should be responsible for bringing the concept to the leadership team with a focus on attainment of goals and the return on investment they will provide.

You will always need your HR team to own the operational and administrative functions of the past. Employees still need to be paid, compliance has to occur and benefits must be accessible. However, you should be challenging yourself and the HR function to ensure these duties are performed in a cost-effective, goal-driven way that meets the needs of the employees and the organization. Your HR executive should be accountable for constant evaluation and options.

If they can't evolve as fast as the workplace, then *FIRE HR NOW!*

MEMO TO HR EXECUTIVES

Our goal with this book is not really to fire HR departments or people. It is to help CEOs understand why HR is such a critical function and why their table is not complete until it includes HR as an active member of the leadership team. In the sections dedicated to the HR professional, you will find tips and tricks for ensuring you are the executive your CEO wants and needs. We do want executives to evaluate HR and set expectations for the business. The goal for HR is that these expectations will open a more challenging and thoughtful career for the HR executives of today and tomorrow.

Business has evolved, and we have to keep pace. HR is an expensive department to run, and while we know the value we add, most executives do not. Most executives have the feeling that all we do is push paper, enforce rules and remind them of all the laws to comply with. They see us as the people who process benefits and ensure payroll is run on time. Managers are not interested in HR telling them all the things they can't do; they want HR to be viewed as problem solvers.

There are a variety of studies that look at what CEOs need their top HR executives to focus on. The issues highlighted do not address the day-to-day administration of HR, but rather how HR can support teams to move organizational goals forward. There is an expectation that all executives will get the basic functions of their department accomplished. When was the last time you attended a management meeting and heard accounting talk about cutting checks, or operations talking about putting inventory away on the right shelves? They just do those things. They come to the CEO to discuss a new way to increase speed of receivables, or the return on investment they will attain with a new piece of equipment. No one wants to hear that you're having a hard time finding good people because we don't pay enough - rather go to the table and talk about the common threads in the best new hires of the last six months - and how you plan to attract more of the same.

When studying the recent literature on CEOs' concerns as it relates to the human capital in their organizations, we see common threads. The list below is a compilation of issues that are common in literature, as well as those that we hear from top HR executives:

- Succession planning
- Finding and retaining top talent
- Diversity communication
- Analysis and forecasting
- Leadership skills
- Change management

Isn't this really what your CEO wants from you? Your CEO is not looking at a list of tasks to be accomplished, rather big picture issues for you to focus on and be innovative. If you do not see your career moving in a direction that embraces these competencies, you have to consider if you are stuck in a rut of administration and compliance. Maybe this is where your CEO and leadership team want you to stay, but if it's not what you want, the book will help you start the conversation with your CEO of how you can add value. As HR professionals, we have to own the administrative tasks, but focus on embracing the needs of our organizations for the future.

There are a number of HR professionals that selected the field because they wanted to be in a position to help people in business. Certainly we have to listen to employees; at the same time we need to understand we are a part of leadership that understands the mission of the organization and helps steer in that direction. That often means we are at odds with employee demands and must participate in and enforce difficult decisions.

Your career aspirations may be focused on the administration and employee service. If that is where your HR career is, there is no judgment, but this book is not for you. This book is for the HR professional who wants to take their department and career to the next level. This book is geared toward showing you what the CEO and executive suite is focused on, and how you can join them.

As the HR executive for your organization, you have to appreciate that business is a series of risk-reward decisions. Only those business functions that impact the organizational bottom line have a seat at the decision making table. And decisions made at the executive level often have a negative impact on employees. Your job is to understand the business reasons behind the decisions and be able to communicate them to the team. You may not agree, but as a member of the leadership team you have to be part of a united front.

Many executives today still see HR departments as a cost center, but we have enormous impact on the bottom line. Articles, publications and research cite budgets that consistently have 40 – 70% of budget line items impact employees and labor related expenses. While this number varies within each organization, the fact remains that you oversee programs and processes that control a huge percentage of your organizational expenditure. You are on the line to make critical decisions that impact the business. If this seems unrealistic to you, the chart below should speak to decisions you make every day.

BUDGET LINE ITEM	HR IMPACT
Revenue	• Hiring top sales talent • Retention of top salespeople • Providing training opportunities to support product needs
Labor Cost	• Understanding and minimizing overtime • Recommending additional hires • Cross Training
Unemployment	• Proper documentation to support claims • Separating employees when in the interest of business unit • Training of managers on real impact of unemployment
Workers Compensation	• Safety Training and Committee • Manage Claims • Aggressively assist with return to work
Benefits	• Understand benefits that attract and retain employees • Provide work life balance benefits that make sense • Contribution strategy management • Administrative functionality • Ensure transparency with payroll to eliminate redundancy
Payroll	• Self service to eliminate administrative HR activities • Constant review of cost of payroll • Streamline activities to eliminate unnecessary functions

If you do see your area of responsibility in this chart, then this is how to approach "the table." HR professionals tend to talk in terms of people, including what and how a new policy or program will make for a better work environment. We need to talk like business people, in terms of ROI and how the top or bottom line will be impacted if we take desired actions. Don't talk to executives about the Fair Labor Standards Act, Family and Medical Leave, time-to-hire, etc.; they just don't care. For example: Let them know you are on top of recent requests for leave and you have forecasted the labor demand with an analysis of overtime pay versus utilization of a temporary labor firm to fill the void. You have analyzed this with the operations team and they agree that the issue can be solved with a financial impact that is still within budget.

Start your conversation about issues that impact management decisions and how your solution will ease the challenges they face. For instance, when determining whether to use temporary employees in manufacturing, don't explain the ease of hiring and evaluation of how the candidate fits in. Instead, talk about the ability to flexibly manage overtime, have a just-in-time workforce, eliminate cost of hiring, reduction in unemployment rate etc. When you approach executives with facts and an anticipated ROI, they will listen. Most importantly, show them you will be accountable for the success of the new project you recommend.

Most organizations today exist to make money in difficult economic times. They do not exist for the purpose of making employees happy. HR is expected to meet the profit-generating goals of the business. In the 1990s, Drs. Robert Kaplan and David Norton published the book, "The Balanced Scorecard" as a strategic management concept in business. In it, they proposed that all functions of an organization must have goals that are aligned with the strategic plan of the organization to be successful. We can embrace this in HR by creating programs that drive business innovation and move the administrative function to the lowest possible level, utilizing technology and outsourcing where appropriate. We must team with the other executives to understand their functional mission and support them through business-oriented programs that remove their barriers. Most importantly, we must use the concepts of the balanced scorecard to reinforce our value and alignment to the leadership team.

HR has evolved through the last century from primarily administrative into a critically important strategic business function. Yes, we still process paperwork, but this can be seen as a training opportunity for entry-level staff. If there is something being done that does not require critical evaluation or does not provide a learning opportunity, find a computer to do it!

HR is expected to meet the profit-generating goals of the business. This book is focused on helping CEOs understand the advantages to aligning professional HR executive with their enterprise. If you want your CEO to be on your team, you've got to be part of the solution, not the problem.

CHAPTER 2

PORTRAIT OF THE HR PERSON

"Start with good people, lay out the rules, communicate with your employees, motivate them and reward them. If you do all those things effectively, you can't miss."

Lee Iacocca, President, CEO and Chairman Chrysler Corporation

You've likely come across a myriad of HR people, and they general fall into a few categories. The HR population tends to run the spectrum from an administrative paper pusher to a thoughtful, innovative business professional who happens to have a basis of knowledge in HR. Somewhere in the middle, we find the HR managers whose greatest glories lie in rule enforcement and the constant reminder that labor law should guide all decisions.

Successful companies have embraced HR as a critical function within the organization. Where we see the goal of HR alignment within business is when there is an HR executive that holds the title of chief human resources officer or vice president of human resources. This person reports directly to the CEO. In smaller organizations, the title might be director of human resources or administrative manager, but we recommend the reporting relationship be to the chief executive to ensure alignment with the organizational strategy. The relationship with the CEO is critical. HR employees who report to another manager, such as chief financial officers, will have their goals more closely aligned with their boss'. This book would then conclude that HR needs to be focused first on the overall goals of the enterprise, and not just one particular area.

You as the CEO may believe you don't have time for another direct report. If that's the case, it's probably because your current HR executive is not adding strategic value, nor has the background that you require for strategic input. If that's the case, then *FIRE HR NOW!*, and get an executive who is part of your trusted advisor team. The right person in HR will not be a burden, but a peer to whom you can assuredly delegate mission critical situations and use for confidential analysis.

The HR team of the 21st century will include positions that are typically titled "HR business partner." This emphasizes alignment with the operation and takes out all administrative functions. Organizations with the HRBP function have moved benefit administration, payroll, employee questions, and the like to a service center or entry-level employees who typically answer all questions for the employee population. This is generally not with "a personal touch" and often by email. The service center can be internal or external, although most very large organizations (more than 5,000 employees) utilize an external service provider. Whether the service center is internal to your company or a third party vendor, there will be a reduced focus on customer service, and employees are expected to handle their administrative needs through self-service portals. The HRBP focuses on the higher level issues that drive the organization forward and add value to the bottom line.

Integrating the concept of the HRBP at some level will be essential to every organization. The administrative functions aside, the need to manage and enhance the human capital at your organization is critical. Your workforce is likely very diverse. It is common for a business to have a staff with a mix of ages, ethnicities, education, skills, languages, personal obligations, finances and more. They're entering the workplace with issues and motivational criteria driving work. Many managers don't want to deal with all the issues employees bring to work, but it's become a part of the fabric that pulls together the American workforce. Your HR function should highlight the positive differences of each group while being aware of the challenges this presents for management. HR should coach the employee population and provide training and services to embrace the diversity.

In much smaller organizations, an outside consultant can handle the role of HRBP. This is a very positive relationship where an internal team member can handle the day-to-day HR functions, and have access to an outside expert that is intimately involved with your organization as needs arise. We see a number of very experienced HR professionals who have left the full time workforce interested in working with organizations on an "on call" basis.

We would suggest if the captain of the HR ship is anything but a true HRBP, it is time to consider options. All organizations will benefit from a properly staffed and aligned HR department. When done right, HR can bring tremendous competitive advantages to an organization and will be lead by the management team member you would never consider firing. But without proper focus and alignment, HR can be the nightmare waiting for a manager at every turn.

You should be able to describe your HR executive with these characteristics:

- Professional
- Communicative
- Decisive
- Responsive
- Business savvy
- Facilitator
- And, most importantly... Problem Solver

HR executives should be reflective of the culture they're part of and able to speak fluently about the business operation. They should be approachable to all internally, but also be able to separate from the employee population as executives: they must know and understand "the gang" without being a member of the group. Their writing skills should provide a level of communication that demonstrates executive experience, while still being aligned with the internal culture. The communication style should be a top competency and one that is utilized daily in both formal and informal interactions with your team.

Communication and patience are key skills you should see on a daily basis from HR. The HR department will have many internal and external constituents they need to manage on a daily basis. Working with line employees, executives, and the external community simultaneously, the key is to have a flexible yet decisive individual at the helm of HR who can professionally represent your organization. Your HR executive must provide a positive reflection of the organization to the general public at all times. Viewing the position as an executive first, your HR leader is the personification of your organization to the public.

The key issues that literature continues to repeat as keeping CEOs up at night include:

- Retention of top talent
- Compliance with government regulations
- Availability of mission critical skill sets

Do these issues speak to you? If so, why isn't your HR executive coming to you with solutions before you bring the subject up? They need to see the issues, both internal and external, and create workable initiatives to keep your organization ahead of the curve. If this isn't happening for you, then *FIRE HR NOW*! and find a management partner who will take the issues off your plate

WHEN PART-TIME OUTPERFORMS FULL-TIME

An equipment sales organization operates heavily over the Internet and has 65 employees in the office. Its HR manager had come up through the ranks and convinced management she couldn't do it all by herself. She was allowed to hire a full-time assistant. She still wasn't able to get all the work done, and the organization was embarking on extensive long-term succession planning issues she was asked to help with.

Management was told it was impossible. Upon review by the executive team, it was found that she was meeting every employee whim, creating spreadsheets by hand because she didn't trust the computer, and filing documents that were also stored electronically. When she was replaced with a part-time HR resource, employees understood the new direction and had no problem adjusting to the streamlined workflows implemented to make the part-time situation work. Essentially, through a combination of technology and an alignment of the proper function of HR, this organization was able to move from two full-time HR team members, to one part-time HR resource. The strategy that ensured success was an agreement to move employees to self-service technology, utilize reports and technology that was available to HR and have the HR resource focus on the strategy pieces that were critical for the organization to meet its eighteen month goals. The savings in HR salary is being used for training and coaching of less experienced team members to ensure a succession plan to sustain the business into the future.

Is your current HR team still providing data about time to hire, complaining that managers aren't available for interviews, racking up fees with your labor attorney, and more? If so, they are adding to your troubles. Instead, we want you to find the HR executive who can solve your problems and allow you to focus on areas that cannot be delegated. Top HR executives do not wait for you to ask about a situation; they are looking at these critical business issues and coming to the management team with data, recommendations, and solutions.

Ask your HR executive about the top three business issues HR is working on. If the answer is a number of internal, HR-facing initiatives, get a second copy of this book – and fast. The answer should reflect organizational business goals and initiatives that meet the needs of key stakeholders. This will typically be through programs within the scope of HR, but should be focused on the overall business, not the HR department.

HR departments exist for both transactional and transformational functions. To ensure common definition of HR activities, the chart below is used to identify areas of the HR function that fall into the transactional and transformational categories. The key to

HR executives today is that they are able to provide appropriate resources to ensure completion of the transactional list, but spend their day on the transformational side. Your HR executive should be considering a variety of outsourcing options for some transactional activities, and understand the cost-benefit analysis of keeping administrative tasks in-house if that is the decision.

TRANSACTIONAL	TRANSFORMATIONAL
Compliance	Risk/Reward
Open Enrollment	Technology Solutions
Process	Innovation
To Do List	Goals
Reports	ROI, Trends, Projections

Where does your current HR function fall on the list above? The transaction pieces need to be completed by less-experienced team members, and the language of the executive should reside in the transformational space. If you have a one-person HR team, consider the amount of time spent on each side of the chart, and be sure it reflects the goals and needs of your organization.

As we move through this book, we will explore what you can expect from your HR function and how to get it. We'll also provide alternatives if it's something you just don't want to deal with anymore.

But, you say, the portrait of my HR person is just a road-block to getting things done.... then *FIRE HR NOW!*

MEMO TO HR EXECUTIVES

The image of the HR person has changed dramatically in the past thirty years. We started as a clerical function, but today computers can handle most of the work of payroll and benefits. Your primary function should be a businessperson who is in charge of the most costly item on the income statement: labor and benefits. This is an executive-level position, regardless of the size of the organization.

You likely started your HR career in an entry-level, administrative function. Then you were promoted, not because you entered the benefits enrollment the fastest, but because someone saw competencies in you that were valued in the organization. You may have been in another functional area, and someone asked you to fill a vacancy in HR. Typically, the traits you possess include strategic thinking, teamwork, ethical behavior, creating opportunities, communication and problem solving. Your CEO wants to see these skills in direct reports, and you need to determine how you can best highlight these skills and achieve your full potential.

The recent work of David Ulrich of the Ross School of Business at the University of Michigan identifies the 20-60-20 formula within the HR profession. According to Ulrich, 20 percent of us are able to contribute to business success, 60 percent are making progress toward getting into the top 20 percent by contributing to the business, and the remaining 20 percent are either not able or willing to engage in the new level of HR. Give thought to where you are and want to be. You have to take responsibility for your own career, and take action to get to where you want to be.

Due to the advent of technology allowing for more self-service of employees, we can anticipate that fewer HR administrators will be needed to do transactional work in the future. Organizations will value HR professionals who are working within the structure of the organization, providing strategic initiatives, are acting as stewards for change and protecting the corporate culture. HR will always be charged with the execution of the employee needs, but the senior members of the HR team will have to be focused on business issues first.

As an HR executive, you must focus on the drivers of your business, including cost factors, competitors, service, and technology. HR needs to understand the barriers to success and be aligned with strategy to address these issues. It's critical in all areas of the employee life cycle. When evaluating aspects such as pay policy, training programs, and how to recruit, you have to make decisions that are grounded in the best interest of the long-term success of your organization. This should be aligned with the short- and long-term goals.

To be an HR business executive means being on the front lines and thinking like an entrepreneur. As you reflect upon the business in which you work, what do you identify that could be done differently? Be the one member of management who can see past the trees to the forest. Being on the outside looking in can be exactly the type of advocate your executive team is looking for. As the HR department, you typically aren't as involved in daily operations, cash flow, and customer relations as the other executives may be. So, when others are faced with challenges in their areas you can be a business resource able to provide out-of-the-box suggestions. Are you a devil's advocate for the decisions being considered? Be analytical of situations in the organization, speak up and push back respectfully.

Learn to love data and change. Whether we like it or not, data drives business, and change is an inevitable part of long-term success. CEOs count on concrete data to make decisions that involve risk – and all business decisions involve risk. As the top HR person, numbers and data can help propel your career. If you just can't do it, get a great HR information system partner. CEOs have an expectation of actionable data from sales, marketing, and production and it should be no different for you. If you want to play in the executive sandbox, you have to be prepared with data that will predict future success. You must be ready to make claims for change, and then be held accountable to those results. This takes work, and possibly a set of skills and/or competencies you may not possess today.

Change is inevitable, but you will find that data offers comfort. Communicating the message to the ranks is often left to the HR team. Being part of the decision making process, and understanding the data that was considered to reach the next step will help you deliver a credible message that employees can support, or at least understand.

Let's look at recruiting and common data that HR provides. There is little significance to executives in days in referencing time to hire or turnover rate without context. Executives might find the facts you provide interesting, but they can't use the information to make decisions. Rather, consider sharing common skill sets of successful recent hires and then show how HR will create programs to find and capitalize on this talent.

Your solutions may include a new recruiting tool or pre-employment testing. Getting the right people in the right seats more quickly will reduce overtime, increase quality, provide clients quicker turnaround, and more. These are the issues that drive the business. Use your HR lens to solve a critical business issue, and you will quickly be invited to the management table on a regular basis.

Do you love compliance? Many HR people do. But we have to use the compliance argument to help managers accomplish what they need in the eyes of the law. HR compliance is filled with gray areas. To be successful and move up the organizational ladder, you have got to be the HR person who advises and educates, but unless the risk is threatening to the organization, get out of the way. In other words, pick your battles. A common complaint of management is that HR is a roadblock to everything. If you constantly stand in the way of managers' needs, you are sure to find yourself out of most decision making meetings.

The HR executive of today is entrenched in the latest technology and evaluating how it can be embraced to meet organizational profitability. We constantly hear from HR departments that they cannot trust people to do it themselves. If that's the case, get new people! Technology can process a great deal of HR work today. Yet HR is typically far behind the rest of the organization in its usage. If employees cannot figure out how to get through an open enrollment process online, can they really be trusted to use the computer driven equipment in operations, or the accounting system they need every day?

Of course, there are those employees in basic functions within your organization that may not have the ability to handle technology. Solutions can be created to meet the needs of this small group, but don't negate technology for the masses to accommodate the exceptions. HR has a reputation of always seeing what can't be done, and telling managers what they can't do. As a group, we have to overcome this perception and be problem solvers for the business, just as is expected from every other functional area.

Embrace technology as a way to both increase the efficiencies of your department and improve the experience for your customers. Managers want to pull data and run reports from anywhere in the country. Employees want benefit questions answered at 3 a.m. and applicants want to know their status without bothering HR. A simple HRIS can make all of this happen with little ongoing effort by the department. As with any change, there will be pushback and glitches. However, after implementation you'll be able to focus on meaningful projects will create an HR organization that you are proud to lead.

Technology implementation generally costs money. It's your job to convince the CEO why this investment will be good for the top or bottom line. Show the ROI and provide deliverables that you will be accountable for achieving. Your organization approves expenditures in marketing, operations, and finance. Look at how those have moved forward and present your ideas in a similar fashion. Don't be afraid to ask vendors for success stories, spreadsheets and other supporting documents that will help make your case.

Know the business, ask good questions, and position HR as the group that will be the partner to management. Meet the needs of the business and focus strategically on initiatives that can impact the overall goals. Your number one focus is to solve business problems.

This has to be the portrait of the HR executive or you are never going to be invited to lead your organization.

CHAPTER 3

BE CAREFUL
WHAT YOU ASK FOR

"Hell, there are no rules here - we're trying
to accomplish something."

**Thomas Edison, American inventor and
businessman**

As a CEO, you have a number of direct reports who
want your attention. In addition, you likely have a board,
bank, customers, and vendors, to name a few. Adding
a chief human resource officer or vice president of
HR may be another direct report you just don't have
the time for. Your current span of control may be far
beyond the recommended norms. But, as Edison said
there are no rules. You have to figure out what is going
to work for your business, and then put the structure

into place. This may mean more on your plate, but it's what you need to accomplish your goals.

That said, your HR executive will want your attention. The right HR person will expect you to be available for the presentation facts and decisions to approve. Theirs will be another schedule to consider when setting up meetings, and another personality at the annual strategy retreat. HR will come to daily or weekly management meetings and add items to the agenda. Your top HR person will understand the business well enough that they will challenge groupthink when it exists, and add the voice of the employee to executive meetings. Is this what you want?

If you're thinking "no thanks," look at your budget and financials. Who else directly impacts this large a share of the total budget? By recruiting and retaining the right talent, providing development opportunities on new products, determining your compensation and benefit offerings, working with safety to control accidents, HR impacts revenue and expenses at every level. You will find the total impact in areas that HR touches to have a tremendous impact on the organization.

How can you not include this valuable function in the top decision making body of your organization? It may simply be that you have the wrong person at the top of the HR team, but you can change that. It may also be that the HR executive doesn't have the right supporting staff or structure. Create the expectation that staff and structure must be changed, or you will make the change at the executive level.

Your HR executive will expect to be treated as member of the management team requesting greater exposure to your industry and your business. HR should attend industry conferences, represent you on professional committees and participate in the local community. In doing this, a skilled HR executive will increase exposure to your business and customers, as well as gain critical depth of knowledge to bring back to the HR team. This will take resources, both time and money, but will pay off tremendously in the base of knowledge brought to the HR function going forward.

There should be a financial budget allocated for the education of your HR executive. A selective program of business classes might be appropriate. This does not mean you have to finance a full MBA at an exclusive university. Consider an executive MBA or business certificate program that would introduce basics of finance, marketing, and purchasing to the HR executive. These can build a foundation that will create invaluable knowledge for your management team. At the same time, you can create an expectation that the executive will take the content from the training and provide meaningful training programs internally for the rest of your team.

Specifically, this knowledge can be brought back and disseminated to those who have been identified as high potentials for the future. We find that high potentials are generally underserved internally and provide the most critical long-term success your organization needs.

HIDDEN COSTS OF AN HR EXECUTIVE

A publicly traded organization was in a financially challenged position and outsourcing its entire HR function. Its spend on outsourcing was equal to that of an HR executive and a generalist. In the best interest of the client, the HR outsourcing group recommended they might bring in an HR executive who could take on some of the strategic work rather than paying consultants. The CEO said his objection to adding top HR leadership was due to the cost creep he envisioned. He said that an HR executive would need office space, want to travel to conferences, and add communication activities, and that would add to the cost beyond the salary and benefits being discussed. The takeaway is that the organization was meeting the HR strategic component from the outsourcing firm. Rather, the CEO wanted to be creative in how he balanced this need with the total expense.

We often see that the HR function is the sounding board for the organization and executive team. As the interpersonal representative on your leadership team, your HR executive may come forward with information that you would prefer not to hear. Peers at the executive level can trust that the HR executive will listen to issues and situations with an open mind and closed lips. This is a critical function of the HR executive in successful organizations.

A great HR executive will be someone who can filter the messages that are typical of employees in organizations, and encourage those employees who always have an issue about something to move on. This can be a productive role, as long as the top HR person has interacted enough with the other executives to understand who is mission critical and whom you are better without.

Your top HR executive will be the one who needs to sit the CEO down and speak with brutal honesty. This may be more than you wanted when you invited HR to the inner circle, but frank, critical conversations are a necessary part of development. HR needs to be able to tell you what they see, and you need to be open to the feedback.

MEMO TO HR EXECUTIVES

Moving into an executive role is a lot of work. If you are reading this book as an HR executive, we will assume you know HR. You can answer most HR questions in your sleep, and arrive at work with a plan for the day. But business doesn't run with siloed departments. Executives in organizations must interact and collaborate all day to ensure all parts of the puzzle are moving in the same direction. Having a seat at the table will require you to see the whole organizational picture, and ensure that your contributions are harmonious with the greater goal.

If you are asking to move HR into a strategic role, you have to know this will take energy, consensus-building and sleepless nights. You may have to return to school to brush up on accounting or marketing. So why bother?

Being an executive is interesting and challenging. Moving HR from a tactical to a strategic partner in the business will ensure the long-term success of HR in your organization because you will be meeting the real needs of the business, not just getting things done. You will be seen as an executive who solves business problems, and can be counted on to provide valuable insight to mission-critical initiatives.

You will also have to carve time out of your day for other business units. It is crucial that you understand each functional area and the challenges they face. HR should attend departmental meetings on a regular basis, not to talk about HR necessarily, but to listen and learn about the successes and failures others are facing.

Participating at this level will to lead to recruiting, training and creating rewards that drive meaningful results to the business. An added bonus may be that you will hear things that your fellow executive misses while they are focused on their functional area. You can be the "inside outsider" in these meetings that challenges assumptions and ask for explanations of situations they see as standard.

If you have not had formal business training, consider earning an MBA, or attending another business-focused programs. At this point in your career, you can gain HR knowledge through seminars, conferences and certifications. Business knowledge is a critical part of your ongoing education, and now is the time to focus on it. There are many shorter programs intended to get non-business majors up to speed quickly.

These steps take time and energy, but the payoff is becoming a well-rounded businessperson possessing a myriad of options for future growth. This is the HR executive you can be if you want to move beyond the transactional HR position.

CHAPTER 4

DON'T LOSE SIGHT OF THE BUILDING BLOCKS

"Unless commitment is made, there are only promises and hopes; but no plans."

Peter Drucker, management consultant, businessman and author

HR exists for a reason. While we are talking about the advantages a strategically aligned business unit can add to your team, you have got to ensure the basics are in place. There are numerous laws that impact the employment relationship, and they seem to be ever changing.

Your HR executive must have one eye on compliance at all times. While we know HR cannot be a roadblock to success, sometimes HR needs to put the brakes on a decision it feels is just too risky for the organization. The fines for missing even one deadline can push a business into bankruptcy, and ending up on the evening news with your sales manager at a strip club can undo years of effective marketing. You need someone on your team that will know the culture of the organization, understand the players on the team and be aware of situations while they are still in development. A senior HR executive will understand the balance of risk and reward in business and be part of the team guiding you to the right decision.

Your HR executive should hold a professional certification; generally this is the Senior Professional Human Resources (SPHR) or the PHR (for more junior leaders). This demonstrates knowledge of the subject area as well as an ongoing commitment to HR. They should also be encouraged to attend ongoing learning and development with a focus on general business and/or industry education. A great labor attorney should be at their side, and a good HR person should not be afraid to call. At the same time, you need an executive who is confident enough in their knowledge that legal fees paid to an employment attorney do not rival the budget of your whole HR team.

We can all agree that HR spends a large part of the day ensuring that you are not embroiled in costly litigation. Do you realize that your HR executive is responsible for understanding, complying with and implementing all the federal laws below on a daily basis? Then add industry, state and local laws that impact your operation and you will have a view of the web of compliance responsibility HR must undertake.

According to the US Office of Management and Budget, in its 2011 Information Collection Budget, the total estimated cost of compliance with business regulations is $176 million – and that is based on man-hours at only $20 per hour. While this is certainly not all focused on HR, you will find that the HR function spends more time than you would like simply complying with and completing these obligations from the government. And – your HR executive is likely paid far more than $20 per hour.

The most critical laws that HR is faced with on a daily basis are listed in the chart on the next page. And these do not even include the new complexity of healthcare reform, which is unfolding as this book is being written, and the final impact of legislation on HR departments will not be felt until mid-2015. However, we do know that this is a major focus and change for organizations, and something that should be at the forefront of action by your HR executive.

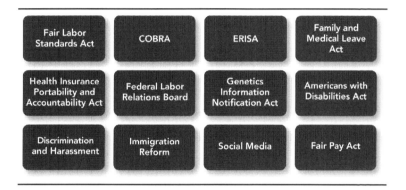

In addition to the compliance side of HR, another essential function is customer service to the internal employee population. Retaining your top talent is a critical aspect of a great HR department, and retention often requires compassion and patience. At the same time, you need an HR team that can determine when enough is enough, and help employees make the tough decision about their position and career within your organization. We will always look to HR depart-ments to be supportive and meet employees' adminis-trative needs as the first layer of the HR operation.

CASH BONUS IF YOU LEAVE

In 2011, Zappos.com offered new hires a bonus to leave in the first ninety days. After four weeks, they asked employees if they want to stay, or take a $3,000 bonus. The company has a clear expectation – employees should evaluate its culture and expectations just as it evaluates the employees. They should determine for them-selves whether they're in a role that's a good fit. While this is certainly an unconventional policy, it is one that speaks to their mission and ensures Zappos.com doesn't put valuable time and resources into an employee that will leave in the future.

Your HR executive must be adaptable and know which issues are worth fighting for. The foundations of your HR function should be in listening, learning and mak-ing decisions. Your HR team must have policies and operate within those policies. But at the same time, it needs to make decisions in the best interest of the business environment. An HR manager who points to policies in the handbook for every decision may not be the right fit for your environment. Policies must exist, but at times they must also be bent, or even broken. For example, consider an employee who loses an aunt. Under most policies, this would not qualify for bereavement leave. The employee comes to HR to explain that his mother died when he was twelve, and this aunt stepped in and provided emotional support to him for the past twenty-five years. The aunt resides in Florida, and there is no one to arrange a memorial event. Do you really want an HR function that quotes the handbook and reminds the employee that no paid time is available for an aunt and that vacation needs to be requested two weeks in advance? Wouldn't it support the culture of your organization for HR to consider the circumstance, speak with the direct manager (who is now a peer of the HR executive) and make a decision in light of the specific facts of the case?

Think of it this way: you expect your CFO to know a debit from a credit, your VP of Operations to know how to run costly manufacturing equipment, and the safety manager to complete the OSHA 300 log, but this isn't what you count on them for. HR must have a deep understanding of compliance, benefits, compensation, training and all the functional areas of HR; at the same time they need to be a thoughtful business executive making decisions in the best interest of your business.

Your HR executive should be charged with building a support team that allows a focus on executive issues, and ensures the compliance and administration is covered. In a larger organization this may be a properly aligned team. In a small organization, there may be reliance on outside resources. But, you say, my HR person gets bogged down in the basics. Then *FIRE HR NOW!*

MEMO TO HR EXECUTIVE

Consider the chart on the next page as the building block of every HR department today. While you may not have the budget for each level, you must embrace each level as necessary to meet the expectations of leadership.

Encouraging you to step up this ladder to a business role is not saying that you should abandon all the years of training and education. You still need to get paychecks written, fill vacancies, verify the benefit bills and maintain employee files. What we do want you to think about is training and development within your own team to allow you the time to focus on the big picture. Consider using technology in every part of the HR function that makes sense to your business. The foundation of HR is still in administration of organizational needs and compliance. You must acknowledge this while being a part of the leadership team that is moving the whole organization forward.

You might be in an operation that is not large enough for you to have a team. Then you should be aligning yourself with strategic partners that can add value and take burden off your focus. Your payroll company should be providing and implementing technology that eliminates needless double entry of data, and virtual employee files so you no longer spend time filing. Your benefit broker should bring all open enrollment documents copied and ready to distribute. If you do not have partners that take the administration of their programs off your shoulders – then do as this book says and *FIRE THEM NOW!*

Many of us got into HR because we were interested in the people side of business operations. Don't lose sight of this. We need to be the face of employees to the executive team. Through meaningful dialogue with employees we find anecdotal situations that we can share as issues with management, and support with statistics. For example, if an employee lets you know that production workers are being lured away to a competitor for 50 cents an hour and the promise of future raises, you can bring this to the next management meeting. But when you do, be sure to bring the turnover rate of the past three months versus the same three months in the previous year, as well as a market comparison of your compensation practices compared with the relevant market. Understand the product pricing strategy of that competitor. If the data does not support the employee's claim, consider an initial communication campaign to explain the long-term employment opportunities within your organization. If the employee's claim is verified but the competition is offering more than your organization can match, consider options such as flextime, training, and culture as reasons to stay with your organization. Use the data as reinforcement to have a meaningful conversation with the executives about their experiences with the turnover, and if they see it as a business issue. If they don't see a problem, move on.

Owning the building blocks doesn't mean that you keep doing things the way they have always been done. The world of business is changing fast, and HR must evolve the same way. When was the last time you reviewed the capabilities of your payroll or HRIS system for functionality? It is common that we find organizations paying for the full suite of services, but only using the tip of what can be provided. Everyone went to system training the week before installation, but who remembers all the functions they introduced you to? We often find reports within the systems that your team doesn't even know are available. Take time every month to step back and reevaluate your own processes. Expect your team to be constantly evolving and creating new ways of doing old tasks.

Oh, and those custom reports! How many hours do you or your team spend pulling data, creating charts and spreadsheets, and sending them to various parts of your organization? Be sure reports you are providing give managers the base of knowledge they need to make decisions. Try omitting one or two, and see if anyone misses it. Consider providing an overview sheet of highlights you see within the report. If you don't see anything of business interest, have a conversation with management regarding the decisions they make that utilize the data of the report. The reports that help make decisions should be available as often as relevant, but if your team is spending time on reports that are just nice to look at, stop producing them!

All task-oriented activities should support the overall mission of the organization. People don't have time to come to a meeting or read an email because you think they should know something. Every touch point with employees should be seen as an opportunity to continue to embrace the organizational mission. For instance, can you use open enrollment as a time to communicate company performance? Is your review process aligned with the characteristics of long term successful team members? Does your employee engagement survey provide opportunities for organizational wins, or just a forum for employees to vent? If there is not a purpose for the future of what you are doing, eliminate it, or find a low touch way to accomplish the same task.

WHAT MESSAGE IS HR SENDING TO NEW EMPLOYEES?

An entry-level employee started at a large non-profit organization. The organization has had the same benefits administrator for decades. On the new employee's first day, she was handed more than 300 pieces of paper. They contained legal documents that needed to be provided, but were not useful to the employee. The forms the new hire needed to complete were placed throughout the pile, and sheets were provided with details of the numerous benefit plans with little contextual explanation. The documents were poorly copied and did not add value to the process of evaluation. On her first day of a new job, the new hire's impression of the organization was that it was antiquated, disorganized and wasted resources. When the 23-year-old employee asked if the documenta-tion was available online, she was told it probably was, but the benefit administrator preferred to give it out in hard copy form. Enrollment for ben-efits was completed by hand and then questions arose based on handwriting and incomplete documentation. The HR team at this organiza-tion seemed to be far more concerned with the process than ensuring the employee was set-tled in, had the tools needed to do a great job, understood the mission of the organization, and had met her team members. The process was not wrong and, in fact, they are quite right in their diligence. It begs the question being asked: was an opportunity missed during the new hire's initial orientation to drive the organization, HR function, or culture in the right direction?

We would never advocate skipping compliance activi-ties; just don't get wrapped up in the details. Be the innovative, action-oriented executive your CEO needs – if it isn't broken, blow it up and find new ways to put it back together! Use this thought to analyze any function today that is laborious and provides no real value to the organization. How can you do it differently to cover the bases and move on?

At a 2013 training session in Chicago of HR professionals, the top issues were still those that we have struggled with for years. The interesting twist is that we saw a slant toward integrating issues with the overall organizational culture. The top HR executives wanted to talk about how to link the HR activity with impact to the bottom line. The top issues the HR executives wanted to address at this meeting were:

- Defining career progression so that the organization is able to attract and retain the best and brightest
- Transforming HR responsibility so that the department is linked to tangible business results
- Ensuring that training lives beyond the classroom
- Cultural integration during mergers and acquisition

As we see in the list, HR is still focused on recruiting, training, and culture. HR responsibilities fall within standard areas of expertise, but we are starting to see a bigger picture view that is needed. In the broadest sense, HR has always been about supporting the organization through people. You do that by engaging team members every day, with an HR team that understands the components of the business. Working with managers, we can ensure that the functional teams have the tools they need to drive the mission. The new link is to understand how tactical functions of HR are driving the organization in the direction set by the CEO.

One goal of this book is to help management understand that the building blocks of the HR function have changed as well. HR has been talking about getting a seat at the table; our goal is to be sure CEOs understand what HR executives can provide. Every other functional areas of the business are expected to be at the table; our goal is to create an understanding and appreciation of HR beyond the world of administration so HR will be invited as a valuable member. However, it's your job to be seen as the HR executive who is not stuck in tactical HR operations, but rather a business partner that can bring a fresh eye to many business conversations. Only by presenting yourself in this way will the other executives accept you as a part of the leadership team. Otherwise missed opportunities are likely to occur if you do not participate in decision making from the beginning.

Ulrich's team presented a Human Resource Competency Study in 2012 that identifies six domains of HR competency. According to this study, The New Skills of an HR Business Partner will need to include:

- Credible Activist
- Strategically Positioned
- Capability Builder
- Change Champion
- HR Integrator and Innovator
- Technology Proponent

These are your new building blocks of the 21st century and you must embrace them, or get out of the way of the leadership team.

CHAPTER 5

HOW TO EVALUATE THE PRESENT

"What is necessary to change a person is to change his awareness of himself."

Abraham Maslow, psychologist and professor

Your current HR executive may have a great relationship with workers and be instrumental in ensuring your low rate of turnover. That's great – there is a role, and an important one, for those activities in your organization. However, that person should not be the HR executive. Your HR executive should be the one that delivers results that help you, as the CEO, drive profits, sales and a future in the direction you want to go.

In thinking about HR teams, we are often asked how many HR people does an organization need. If you have an HR executive telling you they need more people to get everything done, you should be insisting on an analytical reason why this is the case.

To provide a baseline for comparison, we share recent data on HR teams. The ratio of HR to employees remained fairly stable at one HR team member for every 100 employees in the last half of the 20th century. Data from the SHRM Trend survey of 2013 shows that the average organization has 1 HR team member for every 133 employees. The reduction in headcount of the HR function can be attributed to both economic necessity and the technological advances that are available to HR teams in organizations of all sizes. This figure is a generalization for all organizations; your appropriate ratio may change based on factors such as education, location, technical ability, and language of your workforce. The number might also fluctuate based on functions that are outsourced through HR vendors such as payroll, training, and recruiting. Regardless of the use of outsourcing in your organization, the study is still an accurate benchmark organizations can use to evaluate when it is time to add to or decrease the size of their HR teams.

If your organization is smaller than 133, this doesn't mean you can ignore the HR function. We often see HR is often more critical than ever given the complexity of compliance, recruiting, training, and career opportunities. In small organizations, we often see HR as a hybrid function, or a function for which outsourcing is a viable option. We will look at the areas of focus for HR throughout the book, and help you come to a conclusion of how to best incorporate the level of HR that is appropriate for your business.

Averages are just that: the top of the bell curve. You may want a more integrated HR team, or prefer one that requires more employee participation in their own services. There is no right or wrong, but a ratio should be determined that both you and the HR executive are comfortable with going forward. The opportunity this book presents to CEOs and HR executives is to look critically at their HR goals and initiatives to determine what staff ratio is right for their organization.

As we talk about the trend to outsource portions of the HR function, it is critical to remember that managing relationships with vendors takes effort. If you outsource a portion, or all, of the HR function, you will still need a team member focused on the agreement, and able to step in where there are questions or quality issues. This does not need to be a full-time role, but it should be considered that the management of the outsourced provider will take focus from someone on the management team.

We see common themes within various HR functions that are creating large teams. If your ratio is far greater than 1 to 130 for example, consider if your HR executive has embraced and evaluated the reasons why. If you have a much smaller HR-to-employee ratio, consider if the needs of your employee population are being met and the culture you strive for is being driven through the organization.

Previously we addressed that many HR teams have not embraced technology. A large number of HR vendors include productivity improving technology with their products, many of which are included in the price you are already paying. Payroll systems, benefit vendors and job posting websites are three common examples. We see that many organizations with the ability to use digital/virtual employee files still insist on filing paper copies. Having a back-up is critical, they say; creating work for people is what you should say!

Your HR department should be ensuring that the technology department or outsourcing vendor is backing up data on a regular basis and stay away from the paper. We see the same paper-pushing going on in benefit administration, payroll changes, performance management, and more. This can all be done electronically and reduce the need for the HR team to handle paper.

Technology is the wave of the current, and has to be supported by the HR function. In the market today, HR technology should be available to your organization as a part of the payroll and/or benefit function. The translation to significant cost savings across the organization is one that you should expect your HR executive to highlight for you. Implementing technology in any area of the organization is a daunting task, but one that typically pays for itself in the end. Your HR team should be exploring all avenues possible to enhance the service and productivity of the workforce, including the HR department.

The second issue we see is that HR is still guiding the employees through every transaction in the employment life cycle. You may have an HR department that puts a high value on customer service. This is a traditional function of HR, but at the same time you need a group that will teach employees to utilize the resources provided by the organization. This may be the technology referenced above, or it may be the utilization of vendor services. For example, if an employee loses an insurance ID card, does your HR department take care of getting the employee a new one? The employee should be encouraged to call the carrier and get a card, or just print a card off the carrier website. While HR might say it's not a big deal, it will take fifteen to twenty minutes and stop your HR team member from whatever work is being completed at the time. Then there is the additional visit from the employee if the card does not arrive quickly enough, a name is misspelled, or other ongoing issues arise. This is generally accomplished through technology that will enhance turnaround time as well as accuracy for most of the administrative HR tasks. If you want an HR department that drives organizational success, empower employees with self-service as often as possible.

And finally, we see those HR departments that allow employees to use your HR department as a place to "bounce things off" for every issue they have. This takes a huge amount of any HR person's time. While being responsive is essential to the HR function, your HR team must know when to get people back to work, for their sake and your bottom line. HR needs to be accessible to employees, but at the same time should not be spending half the day talking to employees about issues.

Using the chart on the following pages, rate your HR person based on current actions. The action items on the chart are reasonable expectations of the HR executive, and good way for you to benchmark if you have the right person in the seat. Ask your HR executive to complete the same evaluation, and have an open conversation. This book is equally geared to the HR executive taking ownership and encouraging reflection of career aspirations to move into a more significant role for the future. We challenge HR professionals to consider if an executive role is of interest - if not, a decision should be made to move into a role that is more accurately aligned with the long-term career plans and skill set of the individual.

	CEO	HR

	Y Currently does this
	C Capable; but not current
	NC Not Capable
	NI Not interested in HR
	        participating in or
	        handling this
		Y Currently do this
		C Capable; but not
		       currently able
		TN Training needed
		NI Not interested in this

Participate in annual budgeting		
Know the budgeted EBITA and what components are critical for attaining the goal		
Name top 5 customers		
Identify top 3 profitable products or services		
Who are the top three competitors		
What is the top concern or goal of each functional area of the organization		
Evaluate actions for future opportunities		
Know the monthly key metrics and evaluate monthly success		
Collaborates across business units		
Management team is primary work group		
Present needs with data and ROI		
Maintain position and composure when others do not agree		
Participate in lifelong learning outside HR Scope		
Compliance situations are presented with business ramifications rather than "we have to" attitude		
Talk about challenges and ask others outside HR for input		

	CEO	HR

	Y Currently does this
	C Capable; but not current
	NC Not Capable
	NI Not interested in HR
	     participating in or
	     handling this
		Y Currently do this
		C Capable; but not
		    currently able
		TN Training needed
		NI Not interested in this

Spend at least 2 hours per week with functional area team members		
Has spent portion of career in an area outside HR		
Do colleagues go to leader for advice and counsel		
Communication of legislative changes and compliance is with a focus applicable to our business		
Annual goals focused on business rather than HR		
Provides metrics that allow for business to make relevant decisions		
Proactive about addressing issues for employees and managers		
HR Policies are relevant guidelines without being rule oriented		
Training is provided to allow managers autonomy within the law		
Ongoing communication with organization to provide traction for initiatives		
Create opportunities for executives, managers and team members to understand and embody the culture the corporation desires		
Processes are necessary and automated or minimized where possible		

Once you have completed the chart, use the point system below to determine an overall score. The purpose of the assessment is to determine where the CEO and HR executive place the current skills and future aspriations against the questions. It is not an evaluation of a good or bad HR executive, just a way to reflect on the fit with the organizational needs.

	SCORE
Y	6
C	4
NC or NT	2
NI	0

The first analysis should be on the similarity of scores between the CEO and HR executive. If there is great disparity, there may be a misalignment of expectations between the two. This should lead to a critical and frank conversation regarding the expectations of both individuals. A realization may occur that the HR executive can deliver on the skills and abilities the CEO is looking for, or the CEO is not looking for the type of HR business partner the HR executive wants to become.

For scores of 134 or above, your HR person is a true business partner. Consider opportunities to integrate HR into additional areas of the business. You may also find ways to ensure that the other members of the HR team are aligned with the same high-level skills and competencies that ensure a succession path for the future.

Scores of 110 through 133 indicate a need for alignment to the future goals of HR. Have an open conversation about expectations and strengths of HR within your organization with both the HR executive and the management team. Discuss with all managers how having a strategic HR function will serve to meet the needs of the organization as a whole.

Scores of 88 through 109 indicate a need for thoughtful conversation and alignment. You might not want an innovative and strategic function. As long as CEO and HR agree, this may work for your enterprise.

Scores below 88 would indicate the view of HR as an administrative, task-oriented function that can be handled by a fairly low level HR manager, or outsourced to provide ongoing support without executive attention.

MEMO TO HR EXECUTIVE

Evaluate your HR team and your own skill set objectively on the chart above. Every job isn't for every person. This book focuses on changing the vision of HR from an employee-centered customer service oriented department to a business partner working side-by-side with the executives of the organization. While this is a movement of HR professionals today, this may not be your personal vision.

There will always be organizations that are focused on administrative services. The world of HR administration outsourcing is growing and looking for dedicated professionals. There may even be a role embracing these skills within your current organization. If your CEO is looking for an integrated HR business partner, be honest with yourself and make the decision that is right for you. If this doesn't align with your career goals, consider how you can fit into the organization, or prepare for another role within the HR team.

As mentioned above, on average, organizations have one HR professional for every 133 employees. Look at your team and operation. How do you compare? If your ratio is much higher, how are you justifying the additional work? If it is much lower, are you able to provide the insightful data the executive team needs to make decisions that will meet the future goals of the organization? Consider the concepts explored in the book, and be prepared to align your expectations to that of the management team.

Look around at the leadership team in your organization and ask yourself a few questions:

- Are these the people whom you consider your peers?
- Do you want to elevate your responsibilities to be part of the leadership team?
- Is the current team made up of people you feel you can learn from and grow with?

Leaders will be focused on business and put the goals of the business operation ahead of their areas of expertise. When you attend meetings, do the subjects of new equipment, financing and top customer concerns excite you or do you zone out and start planning the company picnic? Considering this will help you evaluate whether the position of HR executive is one that you are even interested in fighting for.

Based on the questions above, see how you compare with the new movement to HRBP. If you are consistently answering "not interested" to the statements, go one step further and consider if you would like to do these things in the future. If so, it's may be an easily solved matter of training and development. If not, it may just not be the right role for you, and you would be more comfortable in a smaller organization with a generalist-type role, or becoming a specialist in an HR functional area. These are equally good career choices, just different from what your CEO might be expecting. Have an open and honest conversation with your CEO regarding your career development and how that fits into the current organization.

CHAPTER 6

SET EXPECTATIONS FOR THE FUTURE

"Not everything that can be counted counts and not everything that is important can be counted."

Albert Einstein, Nobel prize winning physicist

HR will be the first to tell you that a goal must be measurable to be effective - as long as you're not measuring the HR function! Understand that there will be pieces of your HR puzzle that just can't be quantified. But there are HR metrics that will help you assess if the projects and programs identified by your HR executive are meeting the needs of the organization. Einstein said it perfectly: there will be things critical to the HR function that just can't be counted.

Examples of quantifiable metrics include your turnover rate, overtime as a percentage of total salary, the ability to lower the workers compensation and unemployment rates. At the same time, you need to evaluate HR on the softer side of business. This includes the ability for HR to provide guidance and counseling to managers on employee performance, mediating situations between employees, and providing communication that helps drive the mission forward. These are all the expectations you should have from your HR executive, along with the various drivers of your individual vision, mission and goals. Your executive team needs to be in the trenches with employees and have an appreciation that the HR function is providing real value driving the organizational mission.

Considering the overview we've provided, what do you want from your HR team? You as the CEO must make that decision. The HR function will have a strong correlation on employee engagement, ability to meet customer needs and management of a large portion of the annual budget. HR can be done behind the scenes administratively, but you will likely lose some perspective without HR involved in business decisions.

It is now time to ask the $64,000 question:

TRANSACTION OR TRANSFORMATION?

The chart in chapter two shows the activities that are attributed to each side of the equation. The transactional pieces are those that are easily outsourced or handled by an administrative team member. It is the activity on the transformational side that we look for HR executives to embrace. Review the list and determine which side you are on, and where you want your HR executive and team to focus.

Make the decision that is right for the culture and future of your operation. The evaluation should consider the function, not the person currently holding the position. Unfortunately, the decision that is right for the business may require a change in a trusted and valued team member. In reflecting on the role, you will generally find that the transformational activities are those that you need to drive your organization forward. At the same time, you may find that your current HR executive is hoping to move their career in the same direction. This is the best of all situations, as it will be a win-win for you, the organization and your HR team.

As the CEO of your organization, you must be clear with your leadership team as to how HR will be engaged.

While there may be a need for a strategic HR function, there should be associated metrics that drive future performance and add value to the bottom line. Setting expectations of each function is critical, and HR is no different.

When discussing the assessment tool in Chapter five with your HR executive, you may be told how many responsibilities exist around getting payroll out, enrolling new employees, and verifying benefit bills. These are just excuses to stay in the transaction mode. Every functional area has tactical activities that need to be completed. There are basic responsibilities of each functional area and you expect those to be accomplished. Responsible executives understand that activities cannot come at the expense of ensuring they are providing value and helping the organization meet bottom-line expectations. Have the same requirements of your HR executive and you will see transformation at many levels.

Often, we find that HR does not participate in the decision making, so the foundation behind the decision is missing. For example, does your HR executive participate in the annual budget planning, or are they just given a budget and asked to stay within the annual line items? Have HR at the table from the beginning, agree with your HR executive on where you are comfortable utilizing the HR budget, and then let the team run with it.

SOLVING AN OLD PROBLEM WITH A NEW SOLUTION

A large manufacturer in Chicago had turnover of factory workers of 55 percent. HR approached management and said that the interviewing, data entry, termination and general management of new hires was a huge administrative burden. However, the VP of operations said it was no problem: he could train people in three hours; just keep sending people in. HR spent eighteen months trying to get the president to understand the administrative burden in the HR office. The top HR executive attended a manufacturing conference and heard of other organizations utilizing staffing firms to solve a similar issue. With research, HR found a staffing agency that was willing to hire employees for ninety days, and then be hired as permanent employees by the company. HR was able to show that the cost of the agency was offset by the savings of benefits, taxes, workers compensation and administration. The VP of operations was convinced he would gain a more flexible workforce and new hires on demand with little effort. He still trained people in three hours, but he wasn't obligated to keep anyone that was not performing to expectations. They saw it as a win for all, and moved forward with the staffing agency on an ongoing basis.

There is an expectation that training is a critical component of every HR department, but it can also be expensive. According to an article by Laurie Bassi and Daniel McMurrer, "How's Your Return on People?", which appeared in the *Harvard Business Review* in 2004, organizations that invest in training and development outperform the market by up to 35 percent. It is critical that you expect your HR team to own training, development and growth of throughout the entire organization.

A well-crafted development program should include all facets of learning. Your HR executive should not be relying on expensive in-house training or university programming exclusively. You should expect a combination of on-the-job training, mentoring, use of community resources and other out-of-the-box, and often low cost, options. For example, can customer service attend networking meetings to begin to hone their sales skills? Are there avenues for teaching at community organizations that would help your high potential employees develop training skills? Do you reward managers for volunteer opportunities that reinforce management practices and leadership skills? Set these expectations each year and then track successes and failures to be measured as you would all other executives.

Your HR executive is responsible for both embracing and managing the generational opportunities for your management team. HR should highlight each of the workplace generations in a way that adds value to the bottom line and ensures a smooth and productive succession from the executives of today to the leaders of the future. This should occur formally through training and performance management, as well as informally through group projects and mentoring programs. HR should take the lead with the management team to tap into the resources you have, and provide opportunities so that your managers can value and embrace the talent of each generation.

It is common for organizations to have four generations working side-by-side. They each bring a different slant to the work, and we should be working together to harness the power of each group. If the right environment is created and opportunities for sharing and cross-training exist, millennials will learn the work ethic of the baby-boomers, and the baby boomers will learn the speed and access information retrieval from the millennials. We should treat our work environment as an incubator for this type of critical cross-pollination of the soft skills of work.

Many CEOs say they don't want millennials in their workforce – they are lazy, have an entitlement attitude and just don't have the work ethic we expect. But think back to the late 1960s: CEOs couldn't imagine that the hippies of Woodstock would ever show up for work everyday – today we can't get them to leave our workplaces! Millennials bring great skills to the workforce including embracing technology, understanding of a global business interchange and the interest in climbing to the top quickly. These are competencies to embrace, and you should expect your HR team to ensure the values of each generation are celebrated and shared throughout the organization

The performance management process in most organizations is akin to the weather report we all rely on daily. Where else do we see consistent failure and disdain tolerated? It is commonly discussed at all levels of management that performance review processes are a waste of time and don't provide any value. When asked, HR executives are consistently disappointed about the productive value of the annual performance review process. Why is it that the CEOs tolerate this?

If the program is not meeting the needs of the organization, there should be an expectation that the HR executive will change it. It is not your job as CEO to point it out, you need to surround yourself with the type of managers that will see an issue, and come to you and the management team with the solution before the problem is brought to their attention. If the majority of HR managers know it's broken, why aren't they fixing it?

If your HR executive is content with a program that is not meeting a goal or driving organizational behavior forward, you need to consider whether the person is embracing the leadership skills you require from your management team. If not, maybe its time to *FIRE HR NOW!*

A vital expectation of your HR department should be the communication of company vision and mission. Your HR executive must embrace this role both internally and externally. The HR executive is often on the front line with candidates, government agencies, employees and others looking for direction and guidance. Your HR executive must be able to succinctly and professionally describe the organization, its goals, challenges and expertise to the public. HR and marketing should work closely to analyze messaging and create content that will work in a harmonious way with a large variety of audiences.

In June 2013, the Society for Human Resource Management (SHRM) reported the following data in its survey of "Leading Indicators of National Employment."

ISSUES IN HR	INDUSTRY	
	MANUFACTURING	SERVICE
Increased Hiring	1.700%	18.400%
Recruiting Difficulty	−1.200%	10.0%
New Hire Compensation compared with 2012	−4.00%	−2.600%

If you are in a service-oriented business, the chart shows an even more critical correlation for HR to the overall business operation. If there will be an increase in hiring of 18.4 percent, yet it is 10 percent more difficult to find people, what is the plan? HR needs to be looking at this, and not just saying: "we'll place more ads." You should expect a comprehensive solution with action-oriented programs that will get results.

In manufacturing, it may be less difficult for HR to find employees, but are they just filling slots, or are they finding the right people? If they can meet the needs of manufacturing and bring in talent at a 4 percent reduction in salary, that will impact the bottom line. These are the type of expectations that you can have of HR that will move the function from a stagnant cost center to a center of operation that is adding to the bottom line of your business.

Set the expectation with your HR executive that responsibility lies in the soft skills of business, as well as accountability as an executive. In the first year of the new HR expectations, quantifiable goals might focus on demonstrating proficiency in your business outside HR. Goals can be based on acquisition of skills related to other functional areas, attending industry conferences and making presentations to the board of directors. Get HR out of its comfort zone and set an expectation for it to participate at a higher level. The long-term expectation should be that they will be a valuable member of the executive team and able to operate and participate in all business discussions and strategic initiatives.

MEMO TO HR EXECUTIVE

In the 1950s, *Personnel Administrators* magazine had a variety of articles about the need for HR to step up and be heard. It talked about getting bosses to listen to their thoughts and act on personnel initiatives. It said HR needed to fight for their ideas to be heard or risk nothing being done. Sound familiar? We are still fighting this battle more than 60 years later. A focus of this book is to help you get the attention from the executive team that you deserve. You can have expectations for your CEO as well, and we hope that this book empowers you to do just that.

Work with your CEO to set expectations that meet leadership needs, and ensure alignment with the organization, as well as forwarding your own career aspirations. Create measurable goals for HR that are meaningful within the goals of the organization. Understand the constraints, and ensure that the timeline you set is realistic. Now is the time to remember goals which are SMART: *Specific, Measurable, Attainable, Realistic, Time-based*. Work with your CEO to find between five and seven goals that will solve the issues keeping them up at night. Yes, all the other work has to be completed as well, but these are the goals that are going to get you into David Ulrich's definition of the top 20 percent of HR professionals.

The leadership team will not be impressed with your extensive HR knowledge. They want to see that you know the business. You will have to stay current on the issues that are relevant to operations, sales, and finance. To do this, you must understand the context in which each functional area exists. Having a grasp on each of the stakeholders in the business will be critical. Get to know your peers, take board members to lunch and attend other department meetings just to listen. Understand where the financing comes from and be sure you are aligned with those interests as well. Finally, embrace the business strategy in everything you do. The business strategy must be clear to you if you are to drive its basic tenents throughout the organization.

It is a fair expectation that management meetings have time devoted to your critical issues as well. Don't be afraid to shout your issues and pound the table at meetings. While lack of inventory, sales numbers below budget and receivables coming in too slowly are a focus of meetings; your issues are critical to the mission as well. You must give thought to your argument in advance and be sure that you frame the issue with the risk/reward evaluation that demonstrates the overall impact of the situation. If you make compelling arguments supported by data, managers will listen.

Your HR team should follow the structure of the rest of the organization. There should be logic to the various

HR roles, and each role should understand how it supports and impacts the organization as well as their internal customers. HR should be treated as a professional service provider to the entity. A mindset should be expected that the job of HR is not to be an administrative burden, but to ensure the organization is fulfilling their commitment to employees, while working with management to meet the overall goals of the enterprise.

Evaluate your HR tasks critically. Don't be afraid to outsource pieces of HR responsibilities that are transactional and don't provide value to the organization. Embrace technology in all aspects of the employee life cycle and set the expectation with employees that the new initiatives are to improve quality and communication as well as ensure they have access to critical HR information 24/7.

The HR buzzwords in the new millennium are "business partner" and "center of expertise." Both address the expectation that HR teams should be focused on the business, as well as the need to demonstrate deep knowledge in various areas of HR specialization. We see organizations segmenting the business partners from the critical areas of benefits, compensation, recruiting etc. This allows a deep development of talent in the area of expertise, and the HRBP can pull in the appropriate resources as needed for each situation.

If some of the more business-oriented comments in this book scare you, get training – don't just get out. There is also a great career path, with high-level visibility, to be had in a center of expertise of HR. The broad direction of the HR field is creating opportunities to allow each professionals to evaluate their own strengths, weaknesses and preferences and move their HR career in a direction that will be fulfilling and successful.

A great example of the change in HR focus from operational to business is in the case of flextime and telecommuting. If you hear this is something your employees want, don't go to the management committee with the idea that it will help in recruiting and raise engagement score; rather, talk about the ability to reduce office space, operate in inclement weather and serve customers more hours in each day using employees in diverse regions. These are arguments that are substantiated by figures that will be meaningful to managers. Moving to flextime and telecommuting will drive sales and reduce overhead should be the argument. This is what the team wants from its HR executive.

Evaluation is a two-way street. While this book encourages your CEO to evaluate the HR function, you too need to evaluate your CEO. Is your CEO the type of executive who is open to constructive criticism? Is the management team open to a new voice, or do they expect that you will be seen but not heard? You must be able to have your issues addressed without jeopardizing your internal relationships. Is the management team open to this? If not, you'll need to consider what you are really looking for out of the HR function and the future of your career. It may be that your current organization cannot provide you the career path you desire.

You must be able to listen, learn and adapt to the needs of the management team. This may mean coming to the conclusion that the leadership team in your organization isn't the team for you. In most cases, fellow managers will be receptive to your additional insight, and in these cases you can grow tremendously beyond typical HR knowledge.

Your HR team needs a business plan where it can be accountable for results. The plan should show correlation to the overall business goals. There should be alignment between the needs of the business, compliance and the needs of your customers built into the plan. An effective HR plan will show how the HR team is integrated into the overall organization. Expect all members of the HR team to get into operations and understand the business. Finally, the HR business plan should allow for, and expect, innovation at all levels of the department.

Create reports and data that will support the goals. Don't provide your CEO with all sorts of statistics that show your team is doing its job. Create three to five meaningful data points that will tell them how to drive the business. For instance, instead of time to fill a position in recruiting, create a correlation between recruiting sources and performance review scores in the first 90 days. That is meaningful information that you can use to drive better talent into the organization. Everything you measure for your team will drive its performance. The "time to fill" metric will create an incentive for your team to put a body in the seat, and this is likely not the appropriate long-term goal. Rather, consider a metric that would reference the HR team member coordinating recruiting with the score of the new hire on your 90-day review. Successful placements should be those new hires that are successfully integrated into their positions and receiving a good review from their managers.

Managing an HR team is not always an easy job. Often we hear that people want to be in HR because they want to help people. That is no longer the primary function of an HR team. Our job is to put people into positions so that they can be successful and drive the mission of the company forward. Yes, in doing that we are creating opportunities for success among the employees. But it is your job, as the HR executive, to have everyone on your team aligned with the focus of the organizational goals.

By aligning the HR team with concrete deliverables, you will create a function that gets the right people to focus on the appropriate goals. Your HR team needs to understand that their function is about making sure the company makes the goal at the end of the year. They can impact this by hiring the right people, ensuring they are trained properly, and have the tools at their disposal to handle administrative issues without effort during their workday. For the majority of HR departments, this is a new way of operating, and some will choose not to operate this way. As long as you and the management team are aligned in your goal and deliverables, that will define your success.

Think about what you expect from your position, company and career. Ensure that your goals and expectations are aligned with these desires. While the idea of finding a new position can be scary, you spend too much time at work to be unhappy. Be open and honest with your CEO, or current manager, just as they ask at Zappos.com. Chances are slim that they will give you a bonus for your honesty, but you will know if your current role can meet your needs. If not, it's okay to move on. Just be sure to give advance notice, leave good notes behind, and be available if needed. You may not find a position tomorrow, so don't be too bold about your desire for change, but its okay to ask for what you need then take control of your own fate by making a change, internally or externally.

CHAPTER 7

PULLING THE TRIGGER

"Willingness to change is a strength, even if it means plunging part of the company into total confusion for a while."

Jack Welsh, chairman and
CEO of General Electric

After extensive evaluation, your current HR function may not be the function you need to drive the mission of the organization. It may be the person leading the HR function, or it may be the structure and the constraint of the current department. Either way, the first decision has to be made with the most senior person. Maybe a frank conversation will re-align HR, but maybe it is time to *FIRE HR NOW!*

How do you make the change, communicate the message and move forward? The most critical piece is to have your plan in place. The HR function is still critical to the operation, and you want a smooth transition to your next step.

Through your evaluation, you have made the determination of what the next step will be. You should have had conversations with what you need from HR, and honest objective evaluation of the performance of your current executive. If you have communicated effectively, the change should not be a surprise.

You may even have the experience of the incumbent finding a new position before you have to have the separation conversation. However, be sure that you also have your contingency plan in place in the event the incumbent finds another role and gives you two weeks notice. HR is visible to the entire organization, and you want to be sure that the change is seen as one of strength rather than being forced to make a change due to an employee separation.

Most importantly, once the decision has been made, don't delay. There have been countless occasions when a manager has decided to terminate an employee, but waited for the "right time." Then the employee comes forward with a disability, workers' compensation case, or some other issue that will keep them employed with you for life.

THE HIGH PRICE OF STALLING

A financial investment firm had a situation where an employee wasn't performing as well as she needed. Management had a number of conversations with her, yet understood she was doing as well as she could. But the leadership just needed more. Over the course of five months, executives discussed what to do, and came to the conclusion that she had to be replaced. She had worked for them a long time and they felt badly - they knew her family counted on the income. After much deliberation, they decided to do it. That same morning, she came into the office manager and told her that she was pregnant! There was no documentation of the performance issues except the verbal conversation. Appropriately, they called their labor attorney. After deliberation and legal guidance,

> the decision was made that she still needed to go. The agreement - the woman would work three more months, then receive a five month severance in exchange for a release of a future lawsuit. Had they just let her go months prior when they knew they had an issue, it would have saved them eight months salary.

When possible, provide your current HR executive a face-saving exit that will allow for a graceful transition. There are a number of options that will allow an executive to leave the organization with respect. Some of the most common include:

Formal and Visible Transition - Have the HR executive participate in the transition. This will be possible if the HR executive agrees that the future direction of HR is not where their personal career goals are headed. During the planning for change, you can provide time to interview for other positions, as well as help finish open items and leave great documentation of how tactical operations are accomplished. A three- to eight week period is recommended; much longer and you will have a situation that stagnates projects.

Immediate change - In many cases, the HR executive is not on board. Given the bitterness that can exist, and data to which HR has access, you may need to just let the person go immediately. In this case, we would suggest a short period of outplacement services. These services are offered by a number of companies, and the advantage is to have a resource for your HR person. Generally, it is the HR executive who will talk top managers through a separation, but in the case of HR there is no one to fill this role. Messaging is critical, and you will want to ask the separating employee how they would like to handle things, and if they want to participate in the communication. When this is the decision of choice, you should already be prepared with the new solutions for your HR function. Be sure to immediately communicate the change to current team members in a professional way that lays out the plan and goals for the future.

Final Meeting - It may be difficult to prepare for the final conference without asking HR for help. Your information technology team will need to be notified to remove access immediately. You can ask your benefit vendor for assistance, but nothing needs to be completed prior to the conference. Your benefit vendor will likely have a close relationship with HR, and you want the separation to remain confidential until you have delivered the message. At the final meeting, be honest but quick. This is not the time for discussion or negotiation. Your mind is made up, and the changes are in place.

New Resource - It is not unusual to begin the search for your new HR executive before firing the current individual. The advantage of conducting confidential interviews in advance is to ensure you are ready for a smooth transition within such a critical department. As you are having open and honest conversations with HR, you do run the risk that your current HR resource will quit at any time. For this reason, we would recommend you also be evaluating other options at the same time. Where you stand in the hiring process will help you determine how to move forward on steps. If your new HR team is ready to step in, they can be involved in helping with the final meeting as well as crafting the internal communication. If you are moving to a consultant or outside vendor, they should be available to help you with the final communication.

Severance Package - We still see organizations providing one to two weeks of pay for every year of service.

If you provide severance, it is essential that employees sign a release for all future liability. An attorney should provide the release. While it is not mandatory, it does provide protection that can be valuable, especially with the wealth of knowledge your HR person will have.

HR Team and Co-workers - Communication to the remaining team members will be essential. You may have found it necessary to speak with them in advance. Otherwise be sure they are the first people you speak with. You can allow the outgoing HR person to conduct the meeting, but be in the room to ensure that the messaging agreed to is, in fact, the one that is delivered. Generally, there will be questions. You're not required to directly respond – instead, be complimentary of the exiting team member, and state that HR is moving in a new direction.

With constructive change, you will find that your HR function is more supportive and aligned with the organization. Change is always difficult, and the termination conversation is the most unpleasant of management activities, but you know you've done the right thing. Take ownership for the decision, and be clear that the fit does not exist. With proper preparation, the organization will be better off with the right talent in the right seats.

MEMO TO HR EXECUTIVE

If you are reading this book, either you have come to the conclusion that your organization is not providing what you need, or you and your CEO may have had frank conversations about what the management team needs. The decision may be made that you need to move on, and FIRE YOUR CEO NOW! You may have also decided that you need to make changes within your own team. With the many options for you and the organization, now is the time to reflect and do what is in the best interest of all parties.

If you've been having open conversations, don't be naïve: plan for your exit, or start making visible changes in your performance if you would like to stay in the new role. If change is required in your own department and you are up to the challenge, be open and honest about what is required of your team. Find a project or two for a quick and visible win to show leadership that you understand what they need and can make it happen. At the same time, consider what you think of this type of work, and if you want to continue in a role that requires the next generation of leadership.

If the time has come and you have decided to move on, you want to do so with professionalism and dignity. You may have worked with your organization for some time, and it's likely that, regardless of length of service, you have some special and trusted relationships. As you consider the decision to leave, don't let yourself fall into the trap of believing "they can't do it without me." Rather, think about the opportunities for others you are leaving behind.

Documentation is the key to any position, but extra diligence is required if you are planning an exit. As you make appointment entries into your calendar, be clear with phone numbers and contact information. Not for yourself, but in the event that you have an unexpected or quick departure, you want the team you leave behind to be successful.

Be thoughtful and strategic in your exit. Long before you even have another option lined up, consider your team. Who needs what training to move into their next role? Is there an heir apparent who can step in? If so, begin to take that person into your confidence now and involve them in projects, even if they aren't aware they may be completing the work someday. Having a plan for succession will allow you to walk into your boss' office and give notice with confidence. Even if they don't enact the plan you have laid out, you will feel you did what you could to leave the organization in a professional way. It is critical that you conduct yourself as a professional throughout the process. Our business contacts are often prized possessions, and you may need positive feedback from your CEO in the future. You want your exit to be viewed in a positive way so that your CEO will feel comfortable about you as a professional.

If the CEO comes to the decision a change is needed, and you don't have the luxury of timing your departure exactly as you might wish, be professional, but remember your HR training. Listen to what the CEO has to say at the separation meeting, take any documentation they give you and leave professionally.

You might need to have some of the same tough conversations with members of your team that we have encouraged CEOs to have with their HR executives. It's never fun, and not any easier for HR professionals than other managers, but you know it has to be done. It's not always the fault of the employee, sometimes the change in direction isn't a fit with members of the current group. As you would tell any manager, be quick and respectful in your communication.

Taking any of the steps discussed is not easy. Give all options careful consideration, and make sure that the decision you make to move forward is done so `in a way that is comfortable to you on both a personal and professional level.

CHAPTER 8

CONCLUSION

"You can't make an omelet without breaking a few eggs."

By now you have determined what your HR dream team will look like. That may mean that you have made changes in the personnel or changed the focus of the HR department. In either case, it is imperative that the CEO and HR executive agree on what is needed from the HR function moving forward. This chapter is written for both the CEO and HR to consider together, since by this point you have come to a consensus on the way HR will move ahead in your organization.

Literature on the topic of HR leadership consistently highlights the common competencies of an HR executive as:

- Trusted advisor
- Executive, not manager
- Possessing business knowledge in technology, finance, sales and operations
- Innovator
- Vendor Manager

These are the characteristics that your business needs and should embrace. It is up to both the CEO and HR to rise to the occasion and generate the respect for human resources that the whole organization can embrace and understand.

As a starting point for your new HR initiatives, we sum up action items that are a springboard for HR success. These are what we hear CEOs as a group envision as the drivers for business, and how HR executives can be a valuable part of the successful equation.

Be a proactive business leader - HR shouldn't wait for an issue to arise to voice an opinion, and leadership can't wait until it is ready to take action to bring HR into the conversation. HR must understand what is happening in the internal and external environment at all times. HR should be expected to create initiatives that will address the business needs long before there is an issue. At the same time, organizational leadership must involve HR in everyday conversations so the knowledge of employee situations is through ongoing analysis and not crisis management.

Focus on your top and high potential performers - That doesn't mean treating all employees the same. Managers are tired of hearing, "if we did it for Steve we have to do it for Jane." Every situation is different, and HR has to be open to helping find a workable solution for the business. Yes, it is HR's job to be careful of discrimination, but at the same time, some employees deserve more flexibility than others. Listen to needs, consider compliance and provide options. Have a solid business reason for differentiation and allow management to act on that.

Use best practices as a guide, not a rulebook - All executives should be participating in industry conferences as well as meetings that focus on their expertise. Learning about the latest and greatest innovations and practices in the industry will help guide internal decisions. This goes for HR knowing the business, as well as CEOs understanding changes in employee thought leadership. All business people look forward to sharing information and best practices, but it's difficult to treat them as a cookie cutter fit within your culture. You should both use these practices as a launching pad for the innovation around the needs and culture of the organization. Best practices should be used as a compass, not a roadmap.

Understand total compensation - Total compensation is a buzzword in HR, but one that is not always evaluated within organizations. Managing these programs takes time, communication and documentation. Top talent, current and identified high potential employees, has to be rewarded. Otherwise your key talent today and for the future will run, not walk, to the competitor. Pay for performance needs to be integrated into the business language of the future, and considered by the entire management team as a critical component of success. HR can do this with leadership, business knowledge and communication across the organization if it has the support of the CEO.

If the organization doesn't seem to want a high level of HR involvement, then look to the multiple solutions that include outsourcing the function altogether. The idea of a Professional Employer Organization (PEO) is certainly viable. The PEO (or employee leasing as it was called in the 80's and 90's) will take all the administration of HR off your hands. They will provide an excellent benefit program and multiple points of contact that employees can access for help. However, they will not be intimately involved with the organization and assisting with high-level strategic thinking. There is a cost for this service, but for some it's worth the tradeoff of not having to deal with it. Most importantly, it is generally not a cost-savings tool: rather a way to put HR administration in the hands of external professionals.

We also see a new trend emerging in Administrative Services Only being provided on an outsourced basis. In these organizations, the company retains all the benefits of a strategic HR business partner, but outsources all administrative tasks. This can be an excellent solution for middle-market organizations.

There are more and more organizations looking at a hybrid solution where they have the HR business partner they need, but use a PEO, ASO or other administrative vendors for all the tactical pieces. This could be a solution for a business that wants to get HR process completed, but doesn't want to take resources away from strategy to do it.

Having a fully strategic HR function can be an expensive undertaking. Adding a top level HR executive, or giving this level of responsibility to a team member will add cost beyond salary. Your HR executive will want to initiate new programs, need space and an expense budget, and may need to add team members for the tactical pieces of the department. Executives must consider this when looking at the total cost of the HR function, but the value of the HR function internally integrated is far grater than the cash expense when the right team is in place.

There will always be issues in your business operation that impact employees. If you have reviewed the line items on your budget that impact your people, you know that someone has to keep an eye on these expenses. If sales, quality and customer service are drivers in your organization, then having employees ready and able to meet those demands are critical.

Through careful consideration and evaluation, we have provided a forum for consideration to both sides of the

HR puzzle. The goal of this book is to align the needs of the organization with the needs of the HR professional. Only when both sides are in the same place can real HR transformation occur. Human resources is a part of every business, and it has to be addressed. There must be proper alignment between CEO, HR executive and the rest of your organization. Ultimately, you need an executive in the HR function that is going to be a trusted member of your executive team.

Own the need for HR and find a solution that meets the needs and culture of your organization for the future.

Evaluate your current HR talent and needs - and if the fit isn't there, *FIRE HR NOW!*

ABOUT THE AUTHOR

Lori Kleiman is a human resources speaker, author and consultant with more than 25 years of experience advising companies on HR issues. Her background gives her unique insight on how HR professionals and executives can work together effectively to achieve business goals. A frequent speaker on a wide range of HR topics, Lori's programs are designed to provide critical HR updates and best practices to business owners, executives and HR professionals.

Sharing her love of HR with adult learners, Lori is an adjunct faculty member at DePaul University in Chicago and Oakton Community College in Des Plaines, Illinois.

Previously, Lori founded HRpartners, a boutique HR consulting firm that was acquired by Arthur J. Gallagher & Co. in 2007. Lori continued to work with Gallagher for six years to lead the firm's HR consulting practice before branching out again as an independent author and speaker and consultant.

Lori has a master's degree in human resources, has been certified as Senior Professional in Human Resources (SPHR) by the HR Certification Institute and is a member of the National Speakers Association.

She lives in Chicago, Illinois with her husband, and has three grown children.

Learn more at www.LoriKleimanHR.com.

Made in the USA
San Bernardino, CA
22 April 2017